GEOGRAPHY

## Earth 1

# Sun, Earth, Moon and Stars

HERON
BOOKS
K-12 CURRICULUM

At Heron Books, we think learning should be engaging and fun. It should be hands-on and it should allow students to move at their own pace.

For this purpose, we have created an accompanying learning guide to help the student progress through this book, chapter by chapter, with increasing confidence, interest and independence.

Get your free learning guide at
*heronbooks.com/learningguides.*

For a final exam, email
*teacherresources@heronbooks.com.*

We would love to hear from you!
Email us at *feedback@heronbooks.com.*

*Published by*
**Heron Books, Inc.**
20950 SW Rock Creek Road
Sheridan, OR 97378

heronbooks.com

Special thanks to all the teachers and students who
provided feedback instrumental to this edition.

# IN THIS BOOK

# 1

# The Earth

## LOOKING AT THE EARTH

When we go outside, we can see ground and
houses and trees.

As we move away from the trees and houses, they look smaller.

The farther we go away from them, the smaller they look.

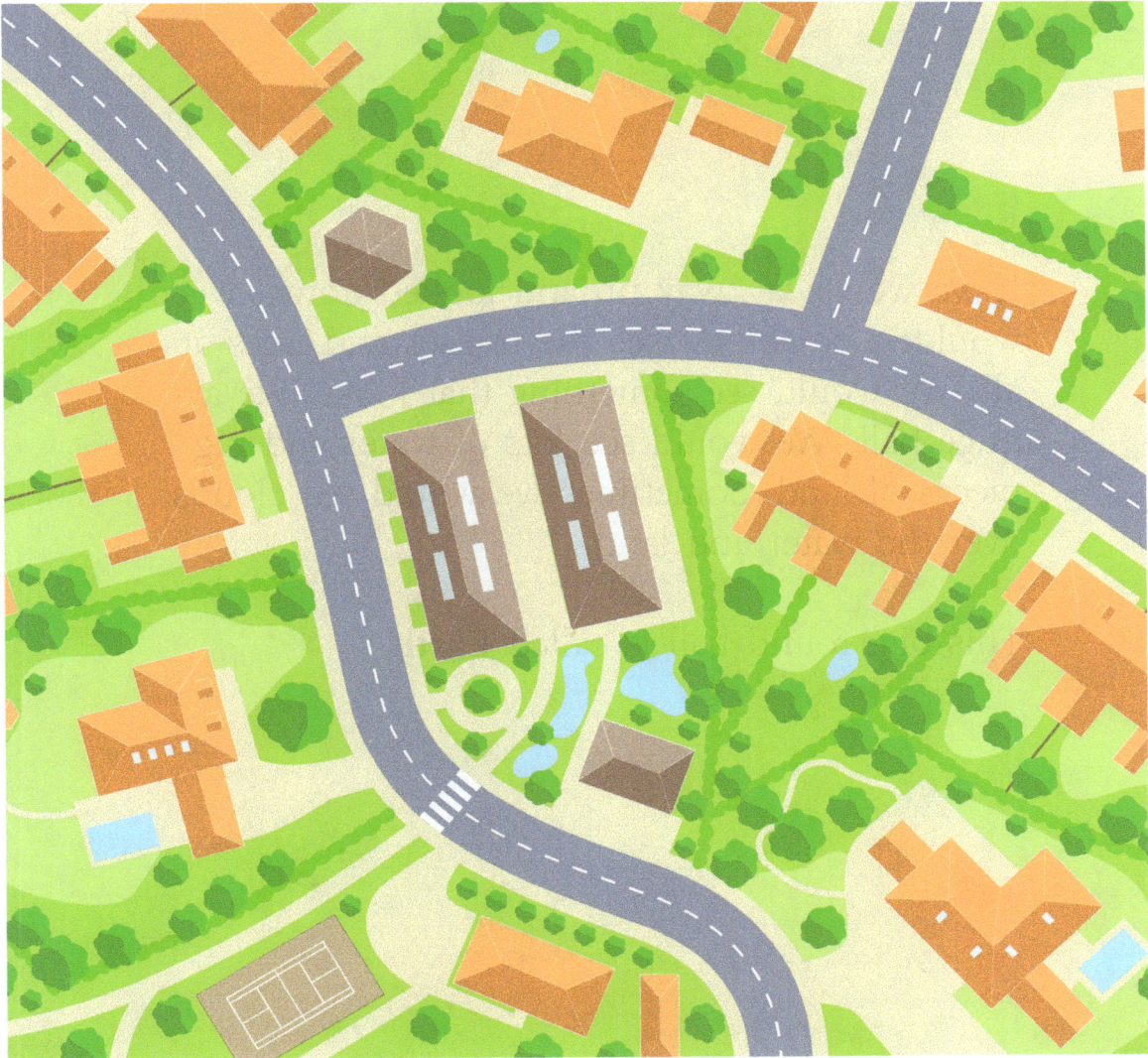

If we went up in an airplane high above the ground, the trees and houses would look even smaller.

If we went way, way up and looked down, we wouldn't be able to see the houses and trees at all. We would see something that looks like a huge ball. We would see lots of water and big pieces of land. Sometimes we would see clouds over the water and land.

This big, round ball is called **Earth**.

If we went even farther away, Earth would look
like a smaller ball.

A huge ball in space like this is called a **planet**. Some people like to call Earth "planet Earth."

There are other planets. They have names like Mars, Jupiter, Venus and Saturn. They are not all the same. Jupiter is much bigger than the others. Venus is hot and Saturn is cold. Some planets are made out of rocks and dirt while others are mostly liquid.

Earth is made out of rocks and dirt and water, and has air around it.

Earth does not look round when we are standing on it because it is so very big and we are so close to it.

## GLOBES

When we study about Earth,
we sometimes use a globe.
A **globe** is a model of planet Earth.

On a globe, the oceans are usually
colored blue and the land is a different
color. You can often find out
things about Earth
by looking at
a globe.

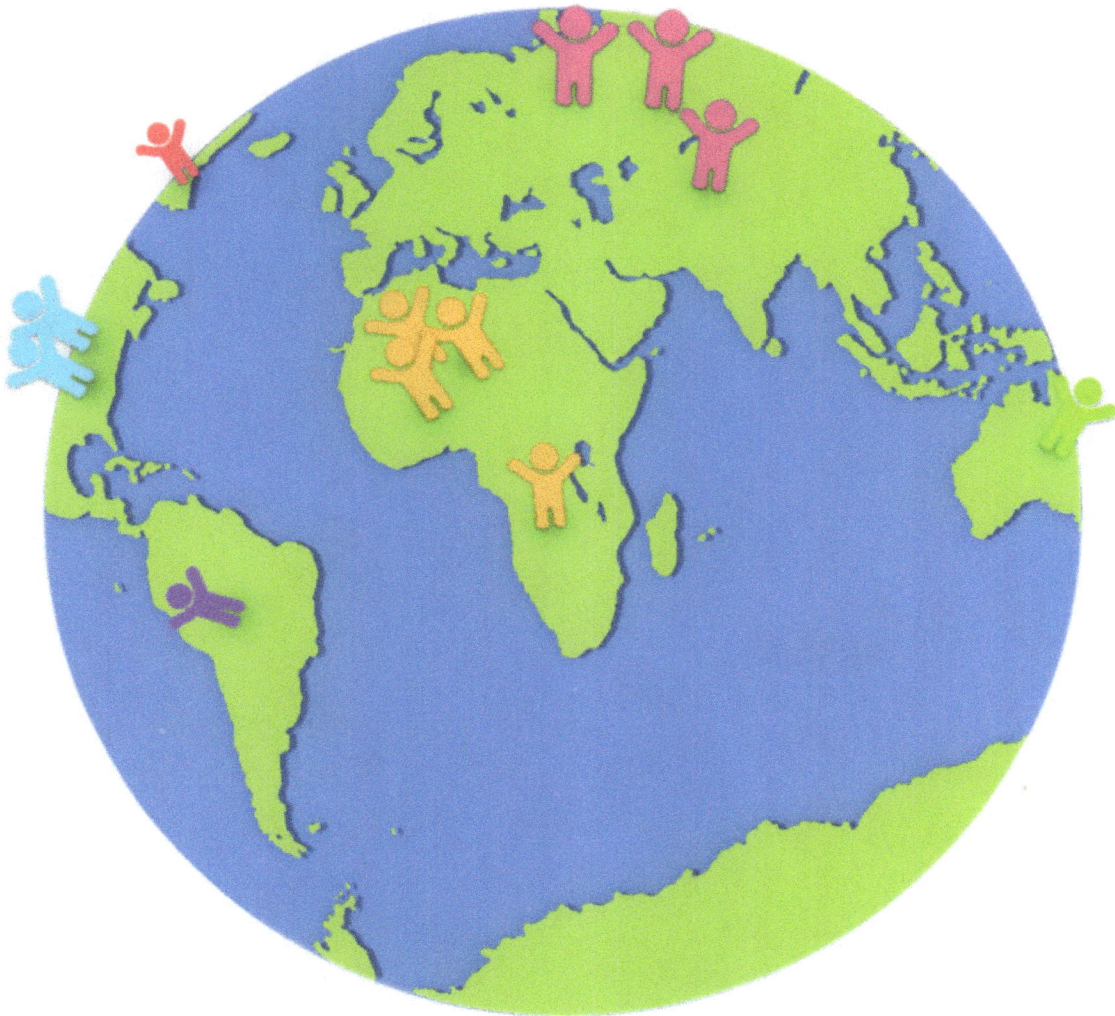

## PEOPLE LIVE ALL OVER EARTH

Many people live on this planet with us. People live almost everywhere on the planet where there is land.

Of course, the people are really much smaller on the planet than they look in this drawing.

# 2
# Gravity

When you throw a ball into the air, it flies up in the air and then comes down. The ball hits the ground, bounces, and stops.

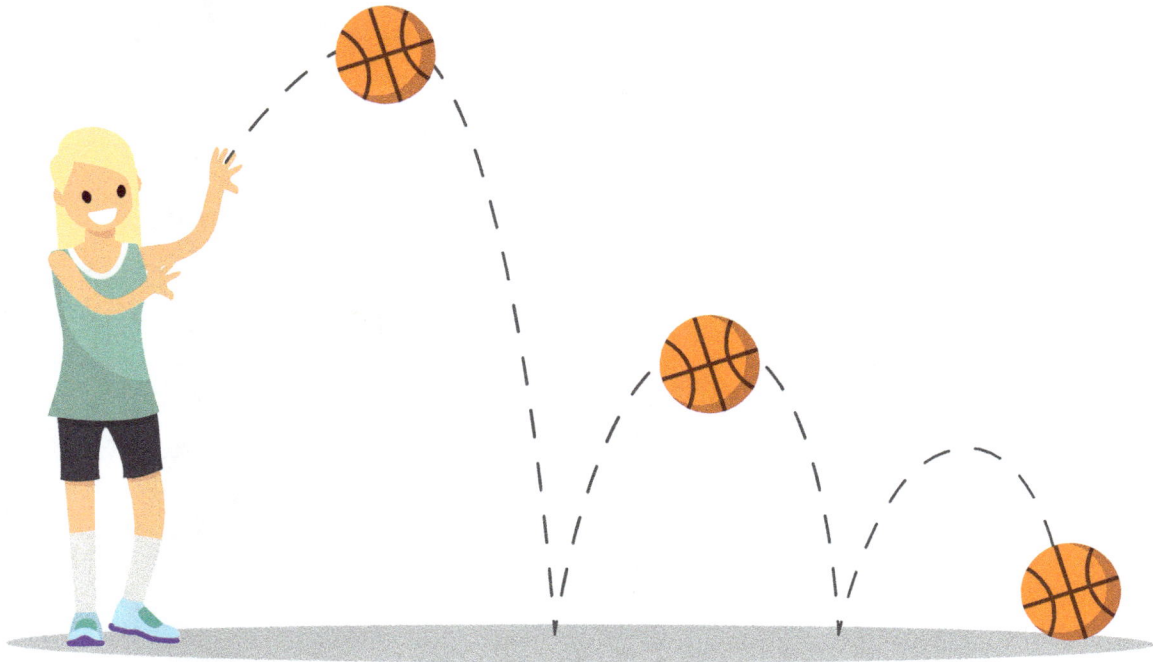

It falls to the ground because Earth pulls everything on it toward the center or middle of the planet. This pull is called **gravity**.

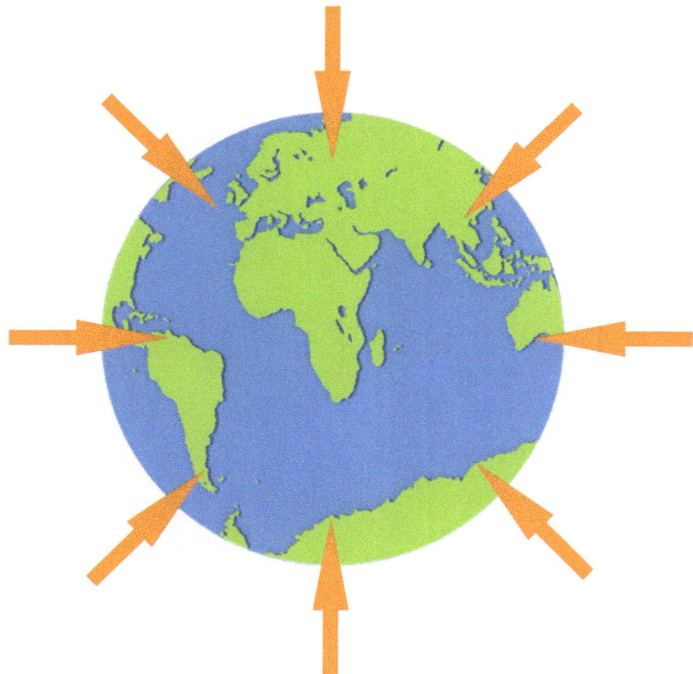

Gravity holds things on the planet. You can see gravity at work whenever you drop something and it falls to the ground.

Gravity pulls on some things more than it does on others. For example, gravity does not pull as much on a ball as it does on a big rock.

When gravity pulls more on one thing than another, we say that thing weighs more. So, in this example, we say the rock weighs more than the ball.

Some things are heavy and hard to pick up. Gravity pulls on them a lot.

Other things are easy to pick up. Gravity does not pull on them as much.

## UP AND DOWN

Gravity pulls you toward Earth, and that direction is always called **down**. The other direction (away from the planet) is called **up**. So anywhere you go on Earth the sky is up and the ground under your feet is down.

When you look at a picture of the planet, it looks like some of the people would be upside down. But, if you went to the places where those people are, it would not seem like you were upside down. When you looked up, you would still see the sky. When you looked down, you would see the ground.

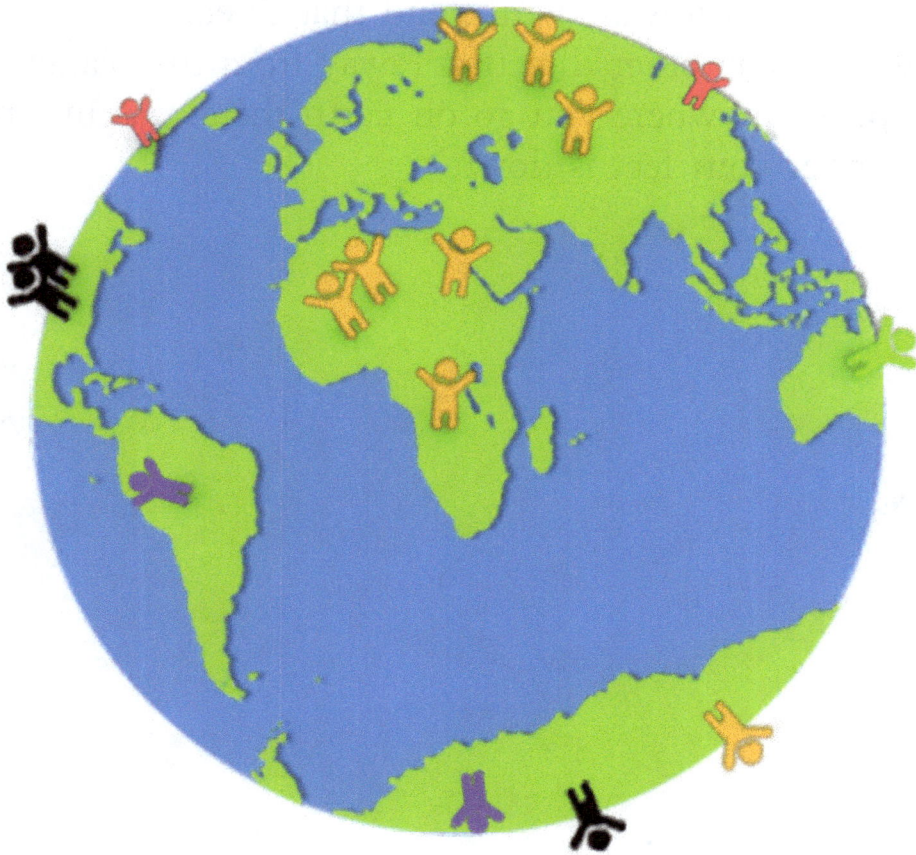

# 3

# Land, Water and Air

On planet Earth there are big areas of land. These are called **continents**. Most of the people on Earth live on the continents.

The Earth also has big areas of water. These are called **oceans**.

There is air around our planet. The air around Earth is called the **atmosphere** (AT mos fear). Our bodies need this air to live. We breathe it all the time.

# 4

# The Sun

The **sun** is a huge, burning ball that we see in the sky during the day.

The light from the sun shines on Earth and gives us light and heat. We can feel the heat from the sun when we go outside on a sunny day. The light and heat from the sun make it possible for living things to grow on Earth.

The sun is much bigger
than the Earth.  It is
very far away, much
farther than it looks in
this drawing.

# 5

# Days and Nights

One meaning of **day** is the time it is light outside.

These boys are playing outside during the day.

**Night** is the time it is dark outside.

## THE EARTH SPINS

Day and night happen because the earth spins.

To us it feels like Earth is standing still, but it is really turning around and around.

Another word for spinning or turning is **rotate**. So we say that Earth **rotates** because it spins around. You can show this with a globe.

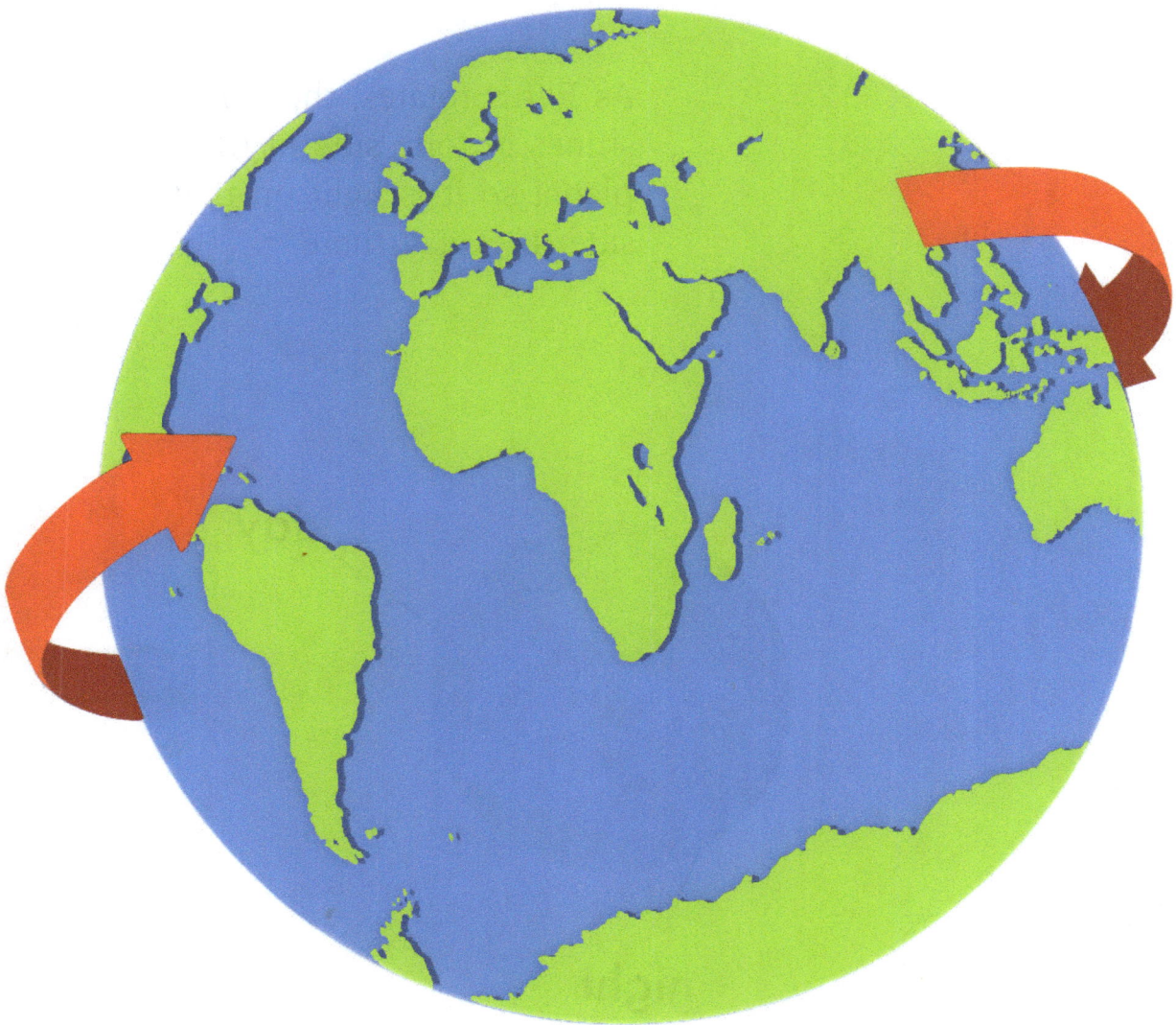

The arrows
mean Earth
is turning or
rotating.

As Earth rotates, the sun shines on one side of the planet so it is light on that side. It is day there.

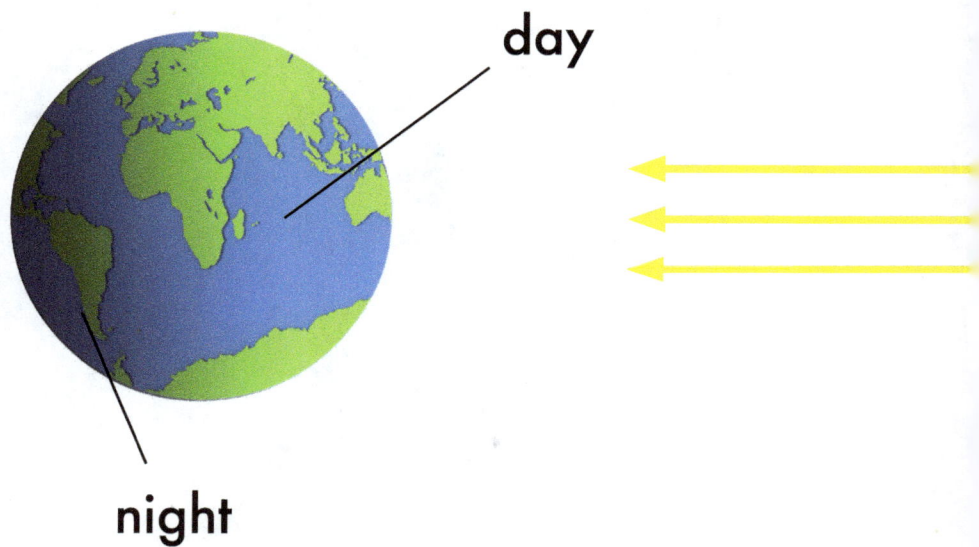

**day**

**night**

The side of the planet that is turned away from the sun is dark. It is night there.

Suppose this is you
standing on Earth in the
dark. It is night for you.

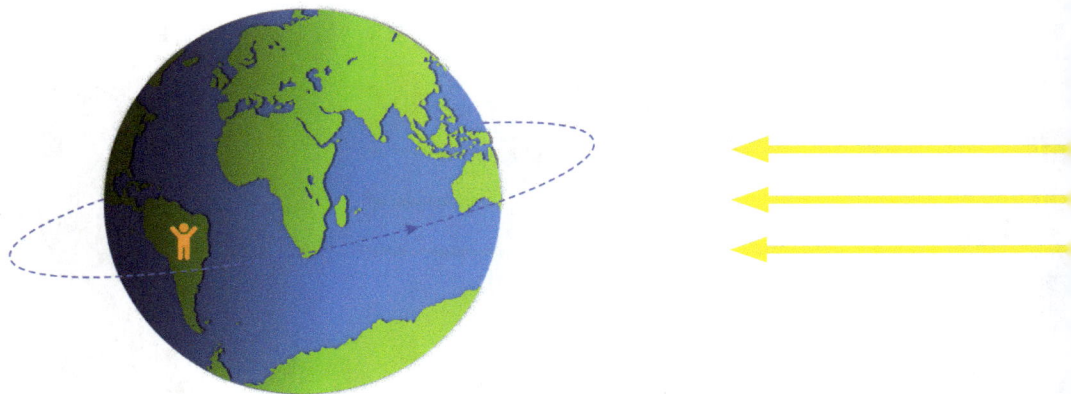

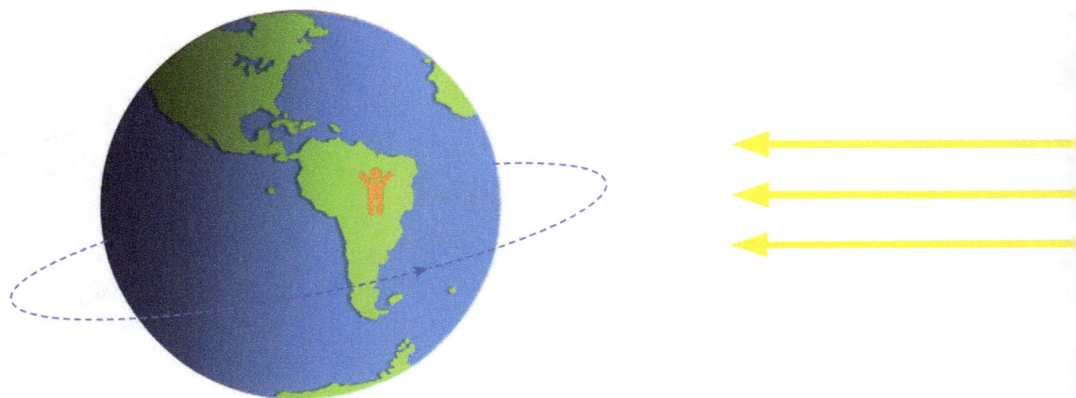

Earth continues to turn and
soon you are in the light—
now it is day for you.

Earth continues to rotate, so night turns to day and day turns to night, again and again. Each time Earth makes a complete turn all the way through night and day is called a complete **rotation**. This takes 24 hours.

This is another meaning of **day**–the time it takes Earth to make one complete turn or rotation.  So, day can mean "the time it is light," or "the time it takes the earth to spin all the way around once."

If Earth didn't rotate, we would not have day and night. It would just stay dark on one side all the time and light on the other.

# Activity
# Days and Nights

For this activity, you will need a globe, a small piece of clay and a small lamp without a shade.

☐ Get a globe, and find where you live.

Put a small blob of clay there to mark the spot.

If you want to, you can make the clay look like a tiny person.

☐ Place the globe and a small lamp without a shade on a table or on the floor.

They should be several feet apart.

☐ Turn on the lamp and turn off the lights in the room.

Rotate the globe so the blob of clay is on the side where the light is shining.

It is day there.

☐ Now slowly rotate the globe to the right until the clay blob moves into the dark.

Now it is night.

# 6

# Years

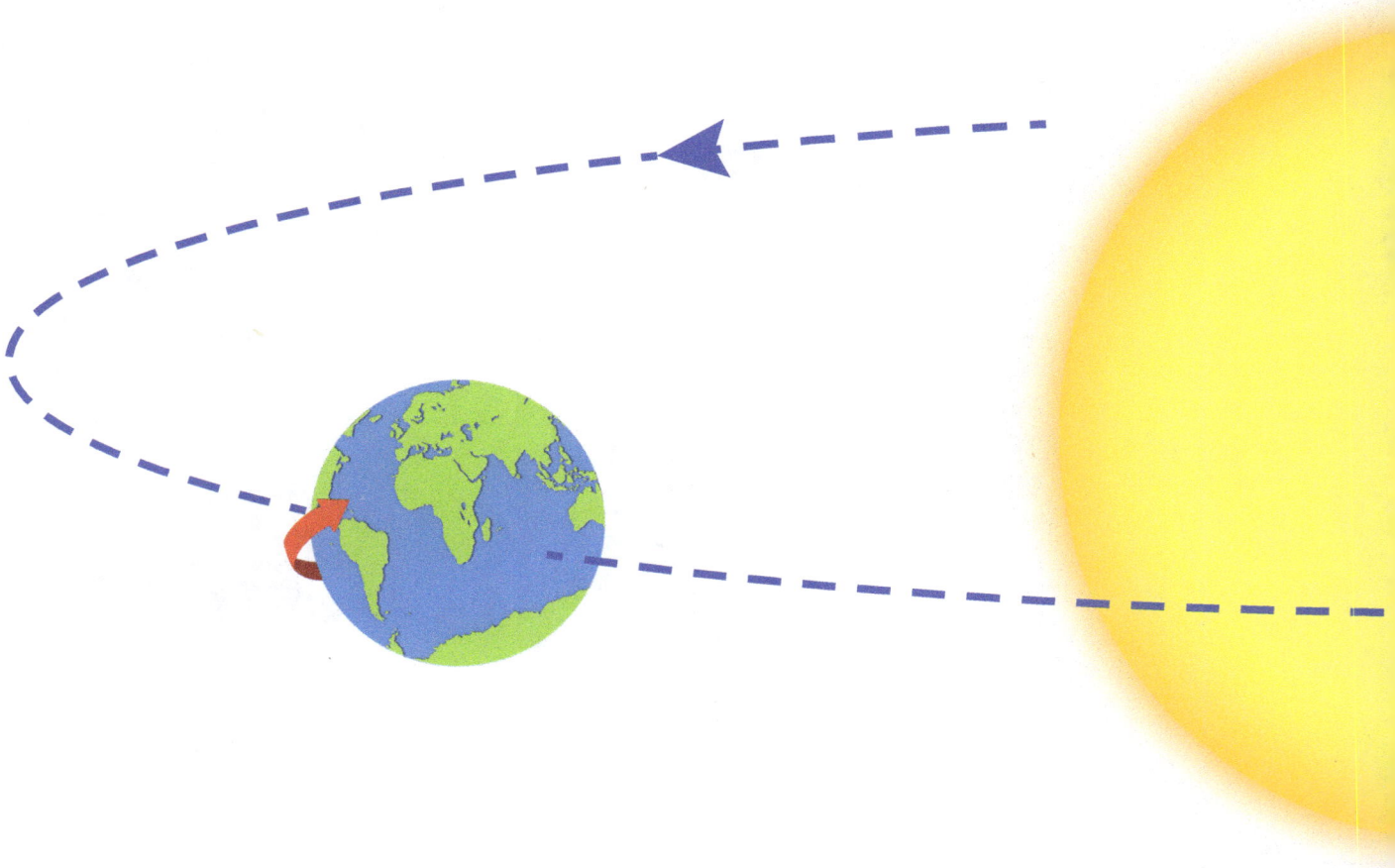

While Earth is rotating through day and night, it is also moving around the sun. It moves around the sun in a big circle.

When we talk about the earth turning through day and night, we say it is rotating. When we talk about Earth moving around the sun we say it is revolving. **Revolving** means "to be moving in a circle around something."

Earth takes a long time to move all the way around the sun. We call the amount of time Earth takes to move all the way around the sun a **year**.

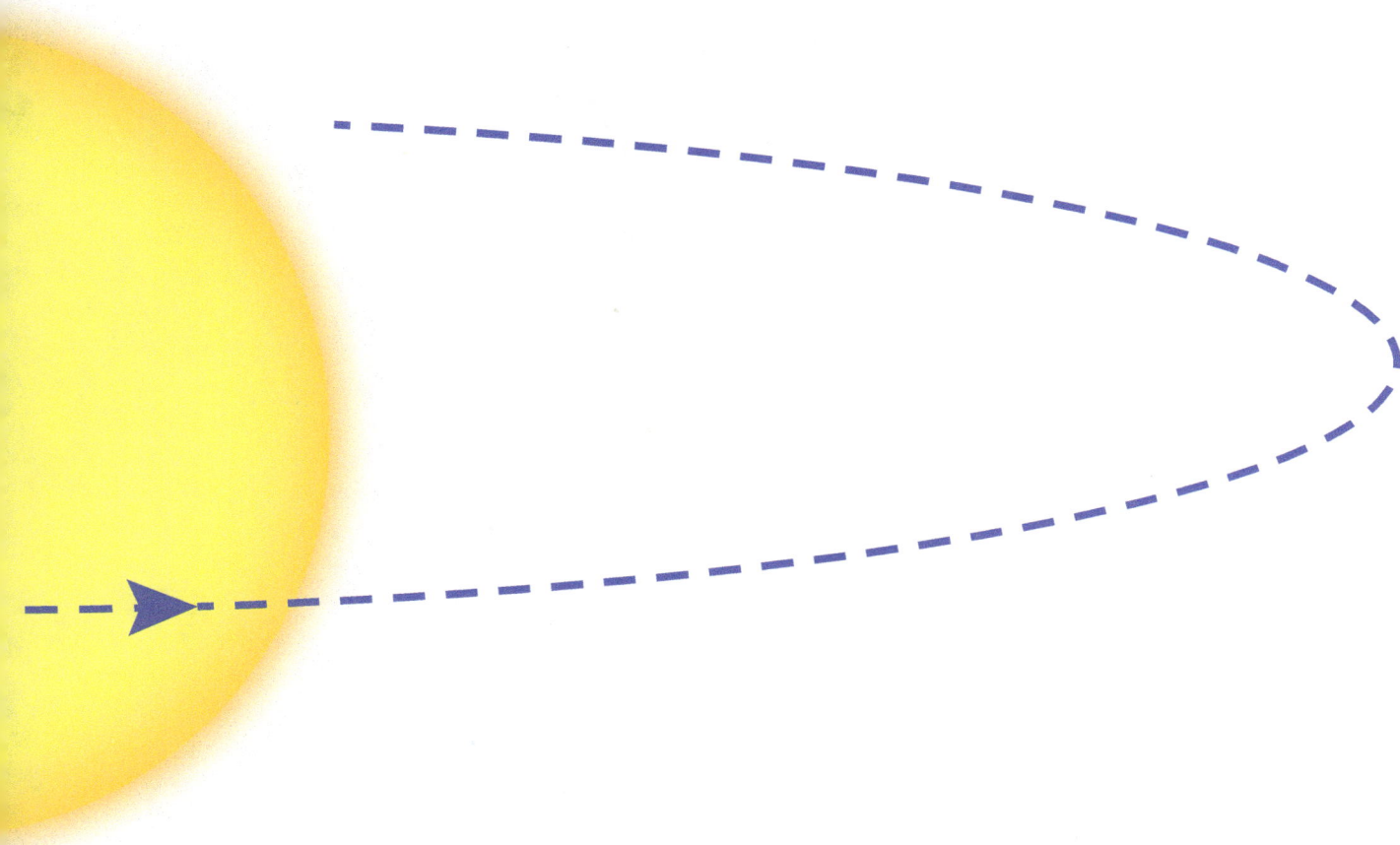

From the day you were born until your first birthday, Earth revolved all the way around the sun and one year went by. So on your first birthday, we said you were "one year old." One more year went by before your next birthday. Then we said you were "two years old."

From one birthday to the next birthday, one year always goes by. That means that between your birthdays Earth has revolved once, or made one whole trip around the sun.

Suppose your birthday
happened when Earth
was here.

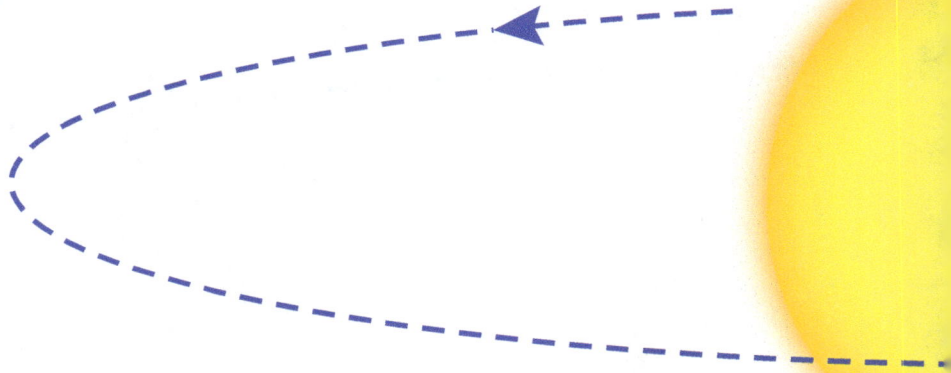

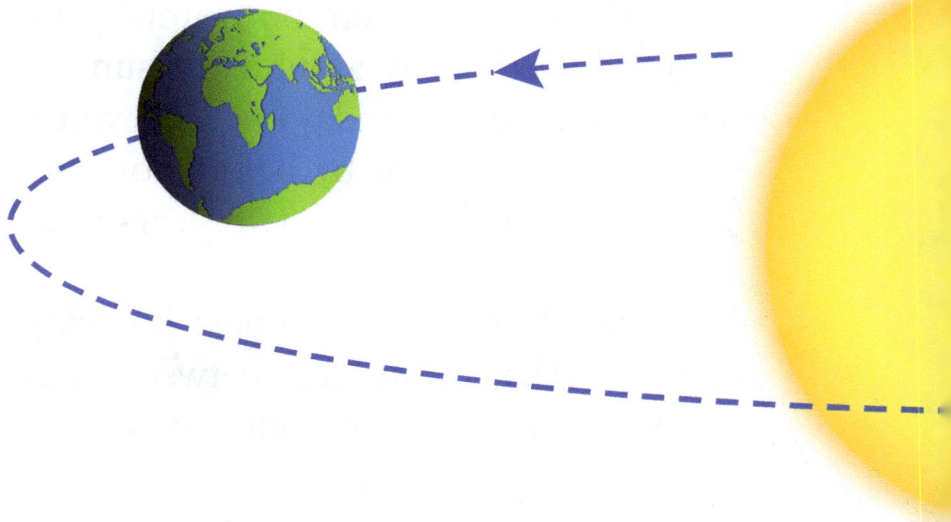

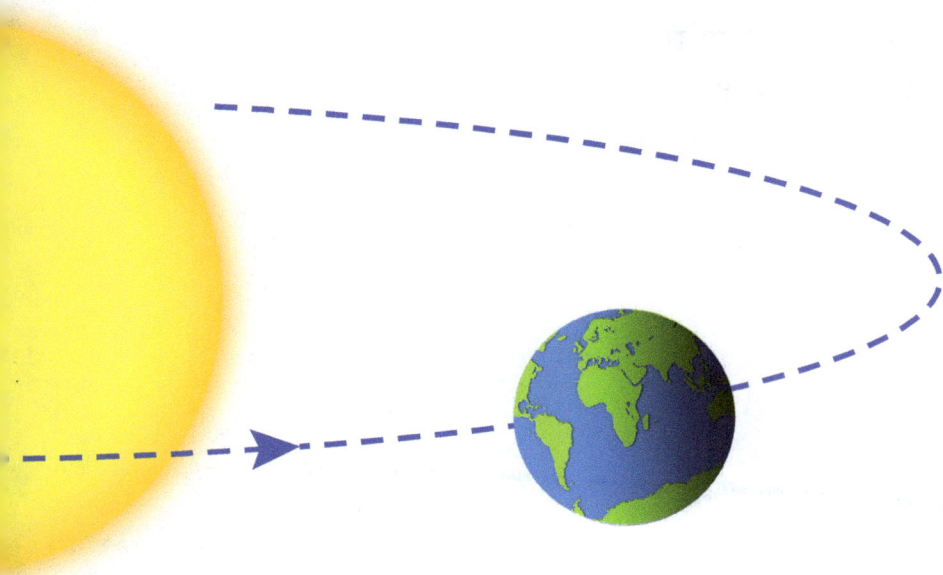

Then part of the year later, Earth would be here.

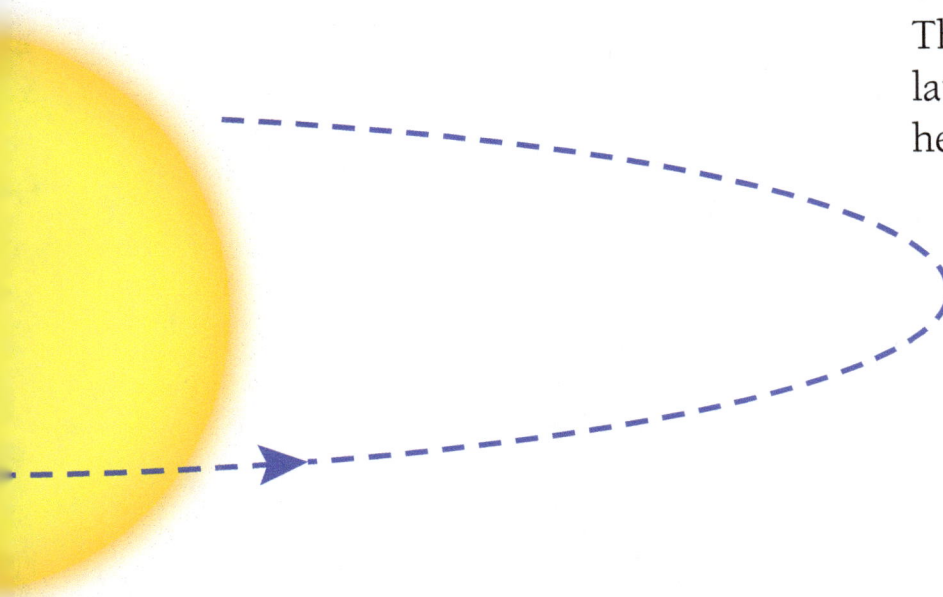

Then when it was your birthday again,
Earth would have moved back here.

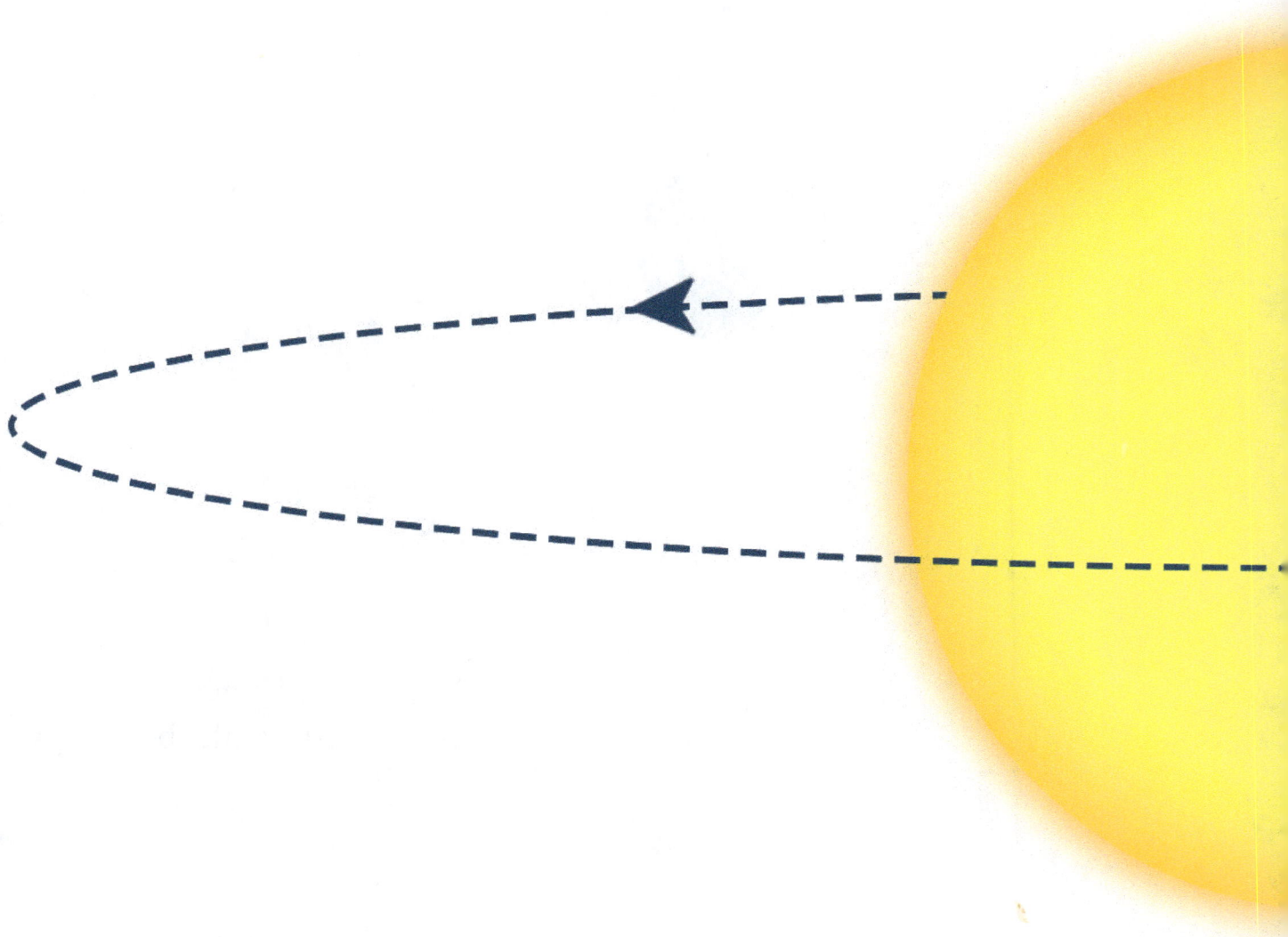

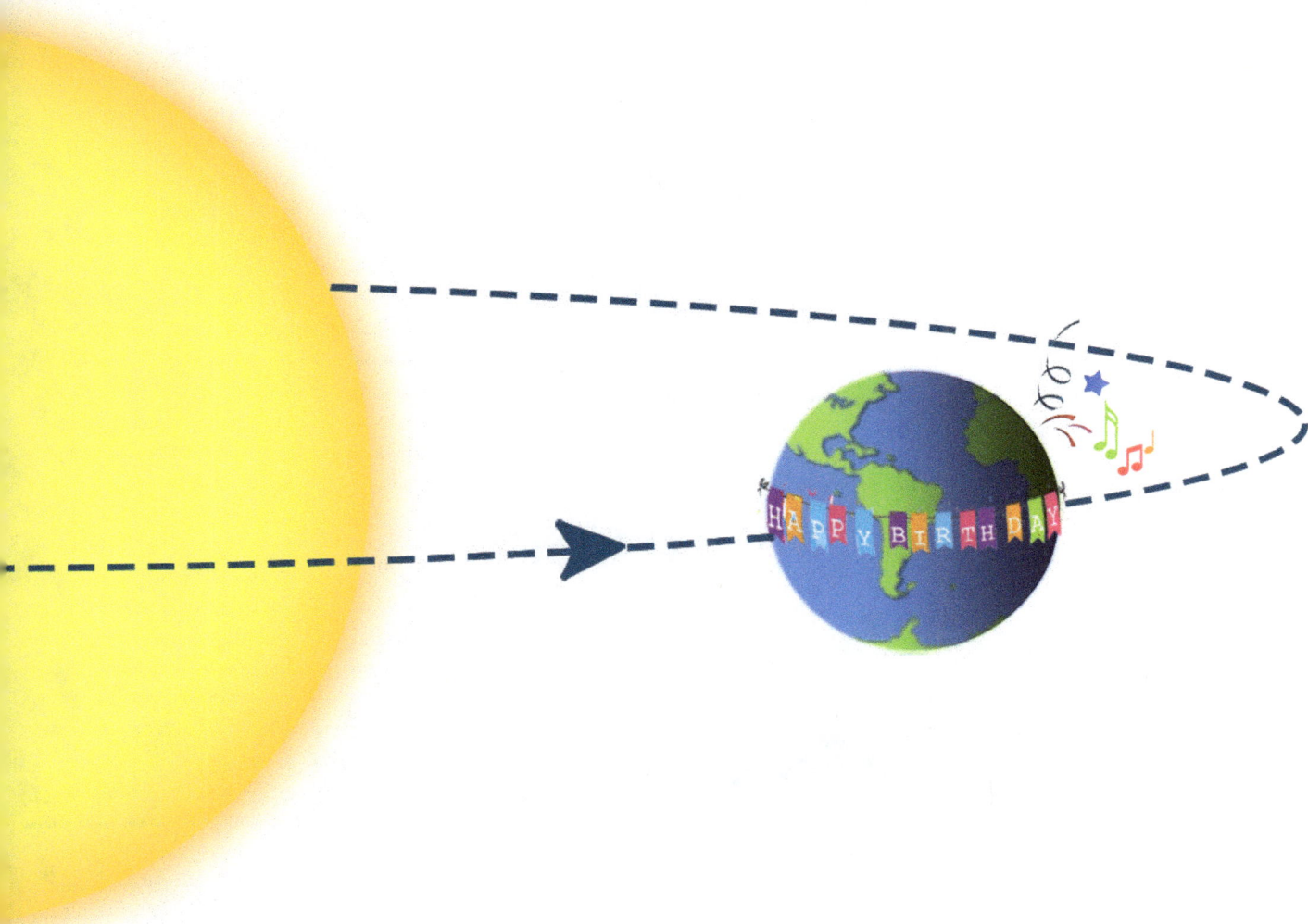

Earth has made one trip around the sun and one year has gone by.

# EARTH REVOLVES AND ROTATES AT THE SAME TIME

So, Earth moves in two ways. It moves in a circle around the sun, or revolves. It also spins, or rotates.

Earth makes just one trip around the sun each year, but it makes a complete rotation every day.

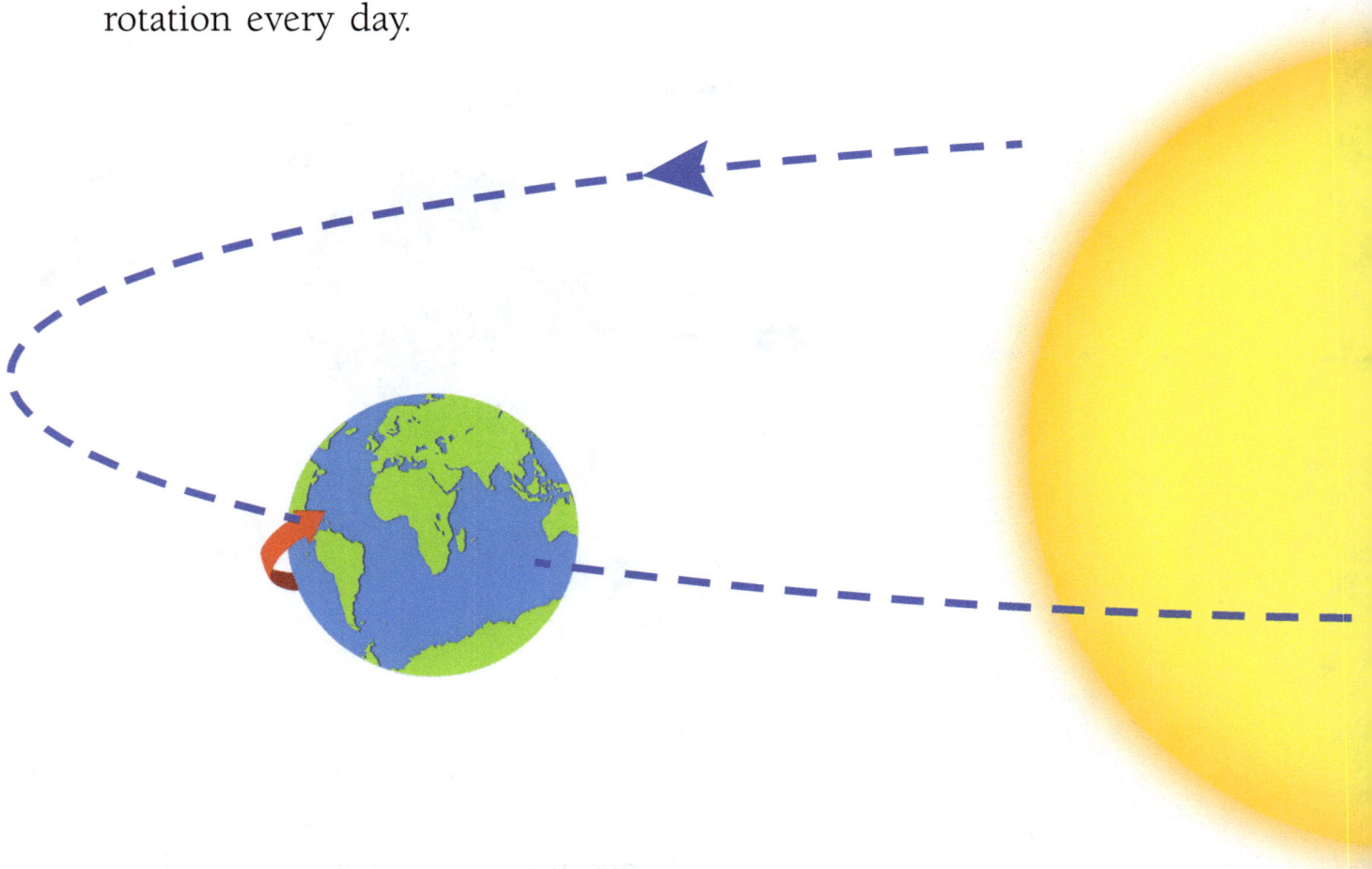

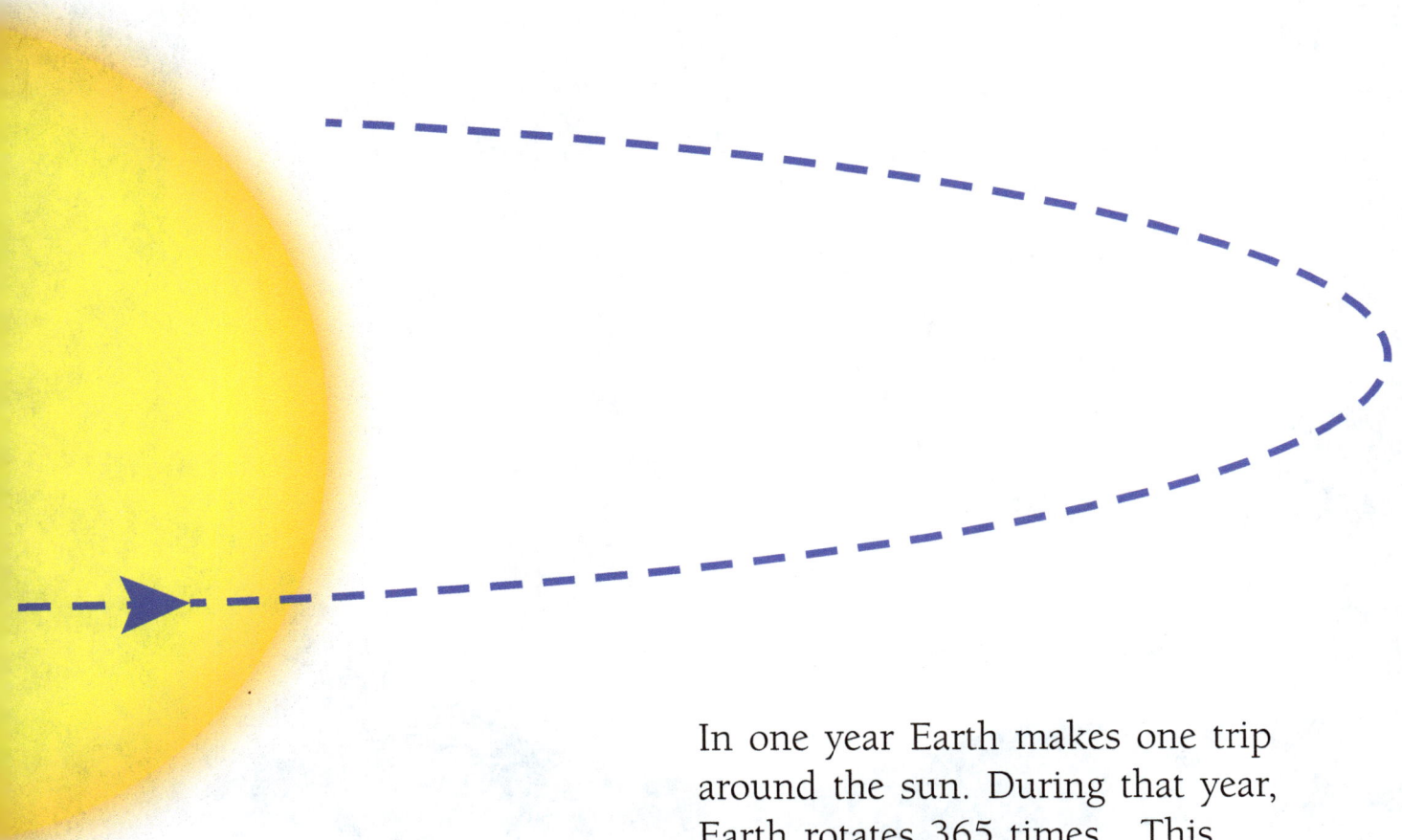

In one year Earth makes one trip around the sun. During that year, Earth rotates 365 times. This means that in one year there are 365 days.

# 7

# The Moon

The **moon** is a large round object that goes around our planet. When we look in the sky at night we can sometimes see it. Once in a while we can see the moon during the day, but it is not as bright as it is at night.

Looking at it, you might think the moon is as large as the sun but it is really much smaller. The moon is even smaller than Earth. The moon *looks* about as large as the sun because it is much nearer to Earth than the sun is. The sun is very far away from Earth. Even farther than shown in this picture.

The moon revolves around Earth while Earth is revolving around the sun.

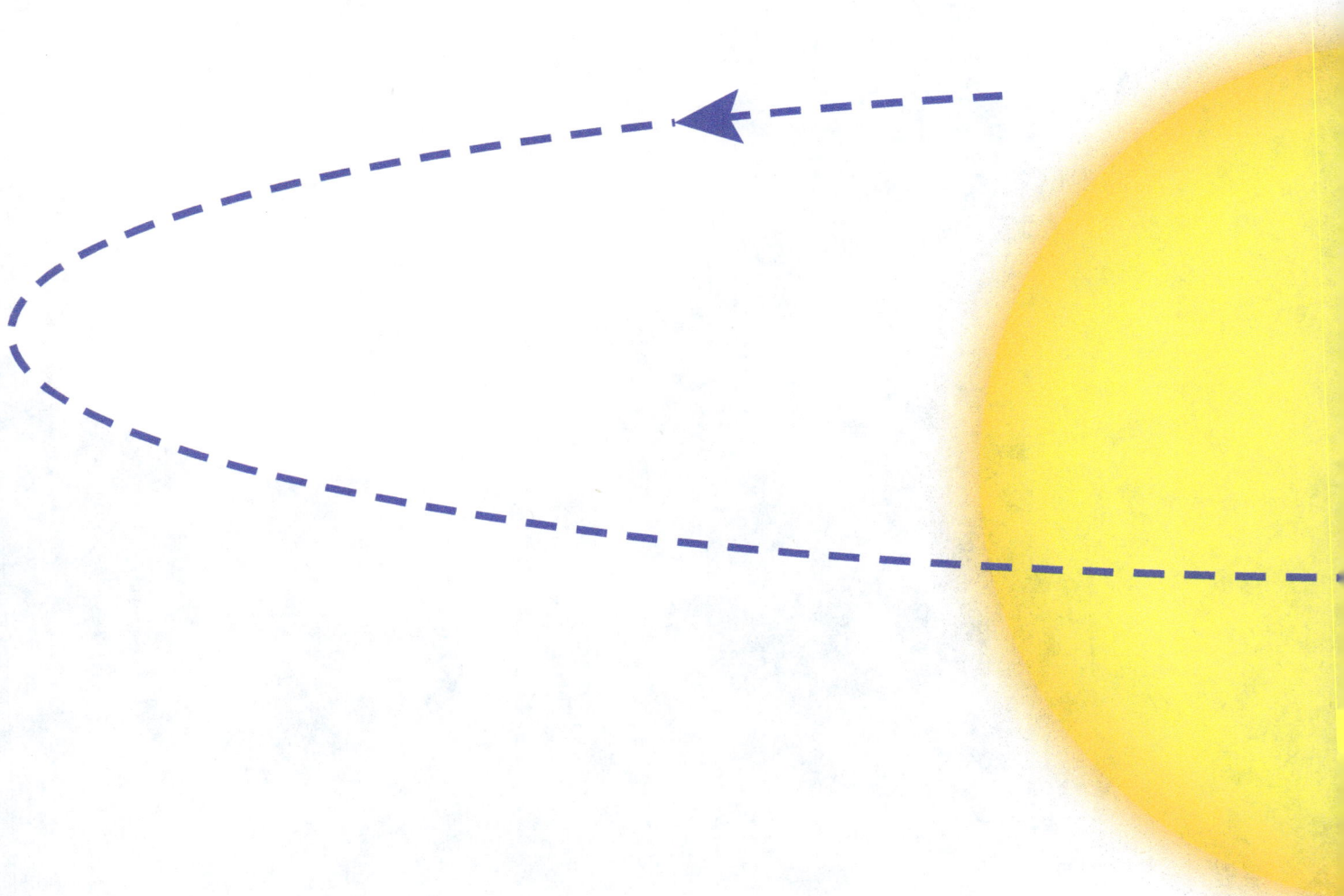

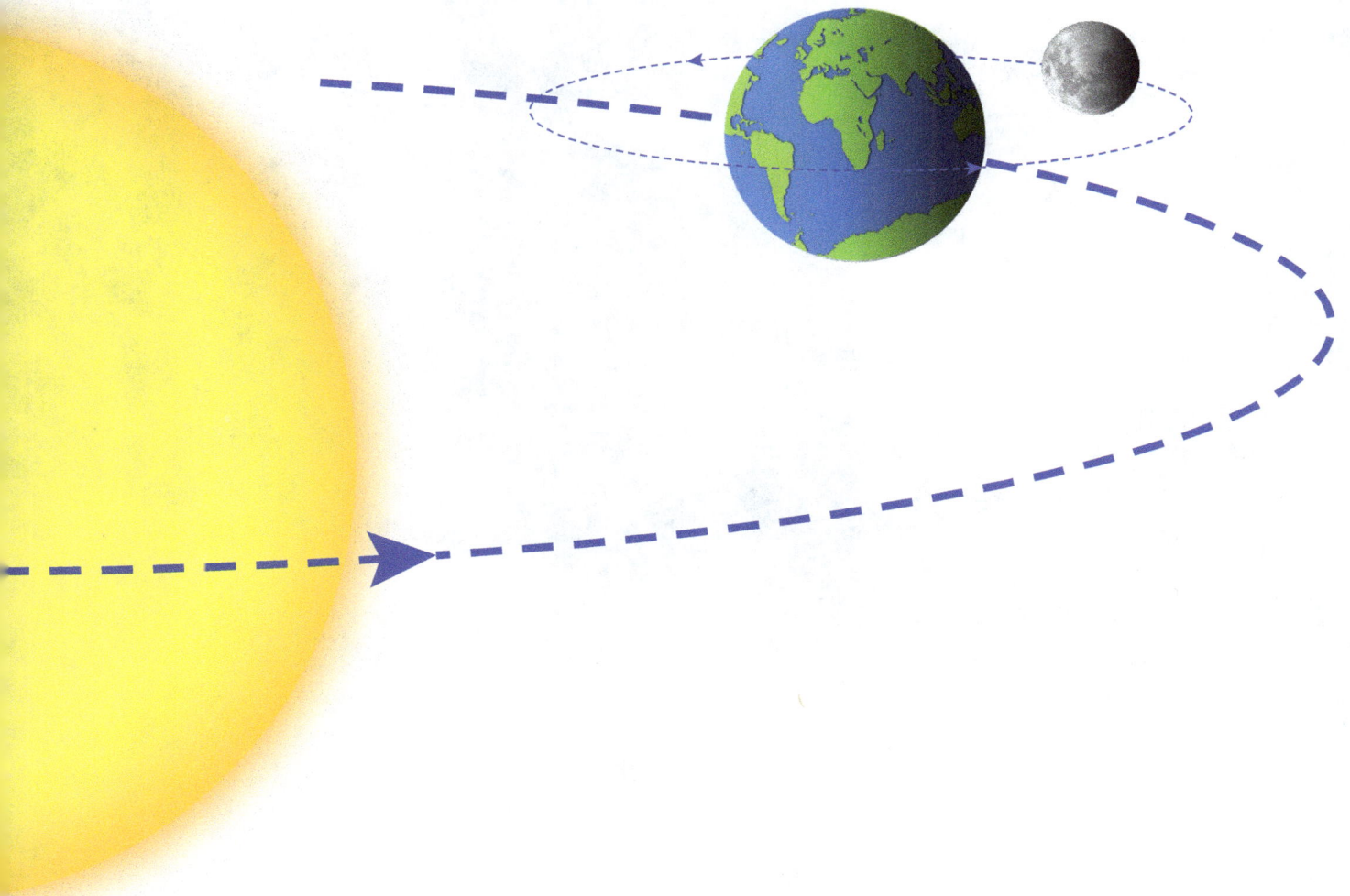

# WHAT THE MOON IS LIKE

The moon is made of rock and dirt. It does not have water or air on it. It is all land. There are many mountains on the moon. There are also round dents on the moon called **craters**. When you look at the moon through binoculars, you can see the craters and mountains.

The temperature on the moon is very different from Earth's temperature. Where the sun shines on the moon, it is very, very hot. Where the sun doesn't shine, it is very, very cold. Even if there were air to breathe, it would either be too hot or too cold for us to live on the moon.

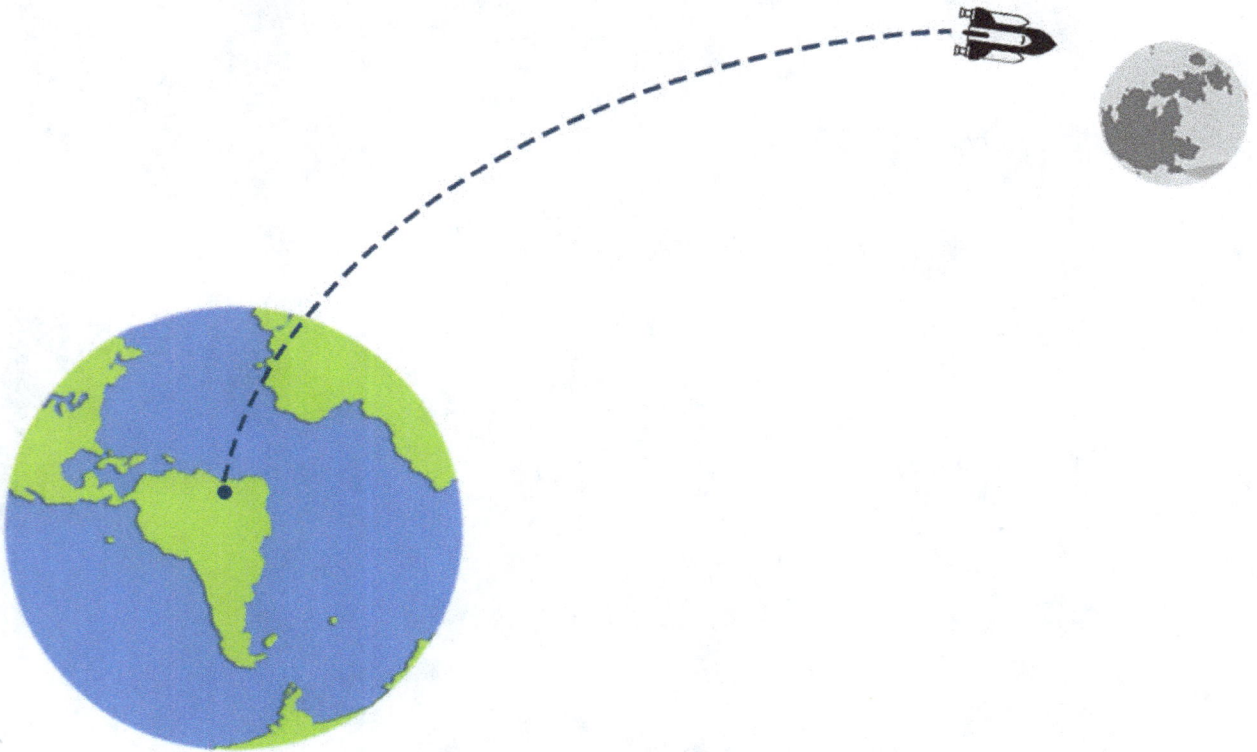

A few people have visited the moon. They made the long trip in a spaceship moving very fast. It took them three days to get there.

The people who traveled to the moon were called **astronauts**. When they reached the moon they were able to walk around wearing special suits. The suits protected them from the heat and cold and gave them air to breathe.

The astronauts who went to the moon took pictures and did experiments so that we could learn more about the moon. They even brought back some moon rocks!

This picture shows the very first spacecraft on the moon and one of the first two astronauts who walked there.

# 8

# Stars

A **star** is a big, burning ball in space. Our sun is a star.

Even though our star, the sun, is very, very far away from us, it is *much* closer than all the other stars. They are so far away they look like little points of light.

The sun makes so much light that we can't see any other stars during the day. The stars are still out there but we can't see them. We have to wait for night when the sun isn't shining around us so brightly and then we can see the other stars.

People have looked at the stars for a long time. Some people have used their imagination when they looked at groups of stars and decided they looked like animals and people and other things. These groups of stars are called **constellations**.

For instance, there are two groups of stars that have been named the Big Dipper and the Little Dipper. A dipper is a big spoon with a long handle. Can you see why these constellations got their names?

You can look at the stars and decide what you think they look like.

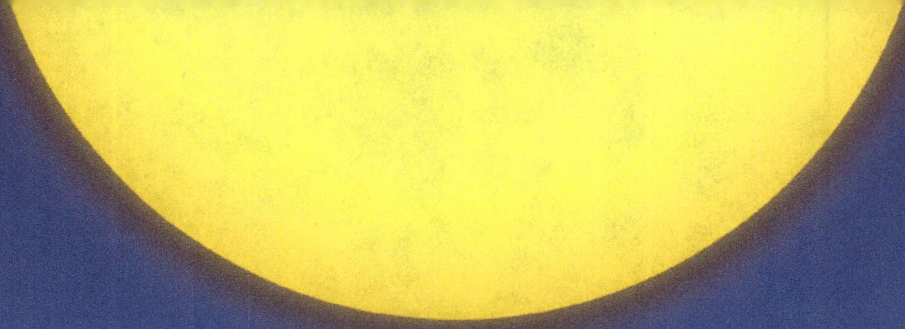

# 9

# Sun, Earth, Moon and Stars

Now you know about Earth, and that it is a big round ball that has oceans and land and air.

You know that gravity holds everything on Earth.

You know that Earth rotates through days and nights.

You know how Earth revolves around the sun, and how that makes years.

You know about the moon, and how it revolves around Earth.

You know that the sun is our closest star.

There are many more interesting things to know about the sun, Earth, moon and stars.

## You have made a great start!